SAY NO TO SUBSTANCES OF ADDICTION

SAY NO TO SUBSTANCES OF ADDICTION

Robert Peprah-Gyamfi

PERSEVERANCE BOOKS

A DIVISION OF THANK YOU JESUS BOOKS

LOUGHBOROUGH, LEICESTERSHIRE, UK

PERSEVERANCE BOOKS
A division of THANK YOU JESUS BOOKS

For information, please contact:
Thank You Jesus Books
P.O.Box 8505
LOUGHBOROUGH
LE11 9BZ
UK

ISBN: 978-0-9564734-7-9

www.thankyoujesusbooks.com

To all tempted to try their hands at some of the substances dealt with in this book; that they may be able to resist the urge.

TABLE OF CONTENTS

PART ONE
GENERAL CONSIDERATIONS

PART TWO
TERMINOLOGIES DEFINED

PART THREE
WEAPONS OF A DREADFUL ENEMY

PART FOUR
TREATMENT OF ADDICTION

PART FIVE
REAL LIFE STORIES

FOREWORD

Dr Robert Peprah-Gyamfi has produced, in this overview of harmful drugs or substances, a very valuable and readable guide. It is especially valuable because it puts the finger on one of, if not the most, dangerous threats to our modern society, as well as the dangers, or minefields, that are easily encountered by the unwary youth of our society, who constitute the citizens of our future societies. At the heart of these dangers is the insidious, and destructive, power of addiction.

Addiction, as our author, a medical doctor, points out, is slavery, because it enslaves the individual, taking away his own power—his *will power* to succeed in life, to become a healthy human being; it takes away his or her freedom, so that he or she is no longer in control of his or her life, severely limiting or impairing the quality of his or her life.

These addictions are pervasive in many societies, in many countries, and seriously destroy or undermine the fabric of society. It is the reason for the increase in crime, since so often the addicted person resorts to crime, often shoplifting, to find the funds to feed his or her habit. The author, who has worked as a doctor in prisons in Britain, is in a good position to meet these unfortunate victims of addiction face to face. So often these are sincere people, well-intentioned, sometimes even from the upper echelons of society (one is even himself a medical doctor), but so trapped and enslaved by their addiction, that they find themselves as repeat offenders.

The book is very thoroughgoing and systematic in exploring various forms of drugs—substances of abuse—ranging from the "softer" substances like alcohol and nicotine, to the "harder" substances such as cocaine and heroin. All this is presented in a very clear, readable, and easy to follow style, often illustrated from examples from the author's memories of life in his native Ghana.

For those already addicted and enslaved to any of the substances mentioned in this book, there is still hope—and this book is very informative about the antidotes and actions that may be taken to free oneself from the hold of the drugs; there are medications and clinics that will help to make the withdrawal symptoms more bearable. At the end of the day, however, the best possible advice is given by this medical author—when presented by the opportunity to try out or experiment with any of these substances, use your free will (while you still have it!) and refuse to partake of these substances that have the power to enslave you. This is a warning that is sounded throughout these pages, and accords with the advice in James 4:7: "Resist the devil, and he will flee from you"—for indeed, the substances of addiction are devilish in their power to enslave and, if resisted, will never have any hold on you. So if offered any of these drugs, do as the author so aptly says in his Introduction: "FLEE, FLEE FOR YOUR LIFE!"

Charles Muller
MA (Wales).PhD (London), DLitt (UFS), DEd (SA)

Diadem Books

ACKNOWLEDGEMENTS

My heartfelt thanks go to God Almighty, Creator of heaven and earth, for imparting the wisdom needed to write this book.

Rita, my wife, together with our children Karen, David, and Jonathan, also deserve my thanks and appreciation for their support and encouragement, which enabled me to persevere to the successful conclusion of this work.

I am also grateful to Dr Charles Muller of Diadembooks.com for carrying out the editorial work and for writing the foreword.

PROLOGUE

NO SCAREMONGERING

I want to make one thing clear at the outset. I am no scaremonger, nor an alarmist bent on spreading frightening information around in regard to the dangers inherent in the use of substances with the potential for addiction, some of which will be dealt with in this book.

Neither am I a sensationalist, comparable to some from the tabloid press who, bent on sensationalism, thrive on the use of exciting or shocking stories or employ language with the intention of provoking public interest, to boost the sales of their book, to increase the possibility of landing it on the best-seller list, perhaps the best-seller list of a renowned paper such as the *New York Times*.

Naturally, it is the dream of any author to come up with a title that will hit the headlines—to strike it lucky like the *Harry Potter* series and gain worldwide readership and enthusiastic fans, some of whom will not mind queuing long hours in front of bookshops, supermarkets and other retail outlets, sometimes in the biting cold of a winter's night, to grasp their copies of the latest in the series of their cherished novel, well before the shops open their doors for business in the morning.

What author will also not cherish the idea of turning up for a book-signing event, to be met with crowds of adoring fans, each demanding the author's authentic signature on a page of his/her newly acquired copy of the author's latest work?

Though I will consider it a privilege to be counted among the successful authors of our age, deep in my heart this is by no means the primary goal or motivation that led me, over the last several days, to spend long hours writing this book, on occasions burning the midnight oil deep into the night at a time when others might be lost in deep sleep, probably snoring loudly or dreaming—pleasant or unpleasant dreams. It was a matter of self-discipline and commitment to sit in front of my laptop pouring out my thoughts in order to come up with this book.

One may believe me or not, but the Lord, whom I serve with all my imperfection, knows from the bottom of my heart that neither profit, nor gain, nor fame is the motivating factor that led me to do what I am doing, namely writing this book.

By the grace of God I have trained to become a doctor, albeit not the very best among my peers. Although I can only dream of the weekly average salary of many a premier league footballer in the United Kingdom of Her Majesty the Queen, I cannot by any means count myself among the least earners on the British Isles. Indeed, while I am not among the quarter-millionaires, semi-millionaires, millionaires and what-have-you of our age, I can nevertheless boast of an income that permits me and my family to live a decent life. Put another way: I do not need to do what I am doing now, yes, writing a book to earn a living.

Why then have I taken the trouble to do what I have done, namely to have produced a book that seeks to highlight the problem of substance abuse with the goal of preventing in particular the youth from indulging in the practice?

After finishing my medical training in Germany, I ended up moving to the UK to work as a locum GP. Allow me to explain the term *locum GP* for the sake of those not conversant with the term. That individual is a doctor, in this case a general practitioner, who usually does not have a practice of his/her own. Instead, that individual has chosen to work fully or partly as a freelance doctor, who assists other established practices to fill short-term shortfalls or vacancies arising from ill health, maternity leave or the annual vacations of the regular staff. One of the advantages of being a locum is that you can divide your time to suit your personal schedules.

One disadvantage of working as a locum GP is what I describe as "no work, no food". Indeed, there have been times when I have been forced to go to work, despite not feeling well, simply because I needed the money that I would otherwise not have earned.

Nevertheless, I chose to work as a locum doctor in order, in particular, to give me the freedom to pursue my career as an author.

Initially the agency I registered with found me work in normal GP surgeries. In the course of time they sent me to work in an unusual setting, namely in the healthcare department of a prison. In time, I was sent to work in various prisons on the British Isles, especially in England. I can count at least ten different prisons in the UK—from HMP (Her Majesty's Prison) Wandsworth in the capital, London, to HMP Hewell in Redditch, a town about 160km to the north- west of London, to HMP Norwich in the east, HMP Hull in the north, right through to HMP Altcourse near Liverpool. My work has not been restricted to male prisons. I have also worked in female prisons, for example HMP New Hall near Wakefield.

In the course of my prison work, some facts that were previously not known to me have come to my notice. These include the following:

17

- Quite a large proportion of the prison population are young adults between the ages of 18 and 30. Of that number a considerable proportion are in prison for illicit drug and alcohol-related offences.
- Of the number serving sentences for drug-related offences, only a small proportion can be described as "purely" drug dealers—by that I mean those caught trading in drugs, who themselves are not drug users. They may give you several reasons why they found themselves in that situation.
- The large majority, at least based on my own observation, of the inmates sentenced for alcohol and drug-related offences, had committed various offences—theft, burglary, fraud, dealing in drugs etc—to fund their addiction.

I do not want, at this juncture, to open a debate on the complex issues of crime and addiction. On the basis of my own prison experience, however, I beg to conclude—you may choose to disagree—that many of the inmates sentenced for drug-related offences are not criminals as such, but *victims* of their addiction.

Another observation I made as a result of my over six years' work as a prison doctor is that once one becomes hooked on drugs or alcohol, or both, it is almost impossible, if not entirely impossible, to get "clean" of the substances involved.

Later I will dwell on the therapy options available for such addicts. Let us take heroin, for example. There are three substances generally in use—methadone, buprenorphine and naltrexone. I do not wish to open a debate on the complex issue involved here. But can we actually regard the prescription of methadone, buprenorphine and naltrexone for people addicted to heroin as a therapeutic strategy in the real sense of the word?

For example, a person suffering a common infection is usually cured after a course of antibiotics over a few days. A person experiencing a common headache can experience relief after a day or a few days' intake of paracetamol or ibuprofen.

That cannot be said of the above substances employed for people addicted to heroin. Some stay on them for the rest of their lives, for the moment the substances are withdrawn they experience withdrawal symptoms that force them to go back to the use of heroin. Quite a good proportion of those on methadone, at least based on the insight I gained interviewing them, still resort to the use of heroin, despite being on the said substance. It may sound brutal, but the saying that "once addicted, always addicted" is not far from the truth—at least based on my prison experience.

The problem of re-offending due to the irresistible craving for drugs is one thing; the direct and indirect effect of substance abuse is another factor that cannot be ignored (more on that later).

Working as a prison doctor, often prescribing methadone and buprenorphine (subutex) in the cases of heroin addiction, and chlordiazepoxide (librium) in the case of alcohol (more on that later), brought me into a personal conflict. Much as I would have wished that the medication I prescribed would lead to the long-term cure of those involved, the outcome of my effort, at least in the short term, was disheartening. For the same inmates I had helped a few weeks earlier turned up again in prison as re-offenders, having again committed crime to fund their addiction. For many of them, it is vicious cycle without end.

In the course of time I became deeply frustrated, as I felt helpless before the huge problem of substance abuse. What served as the proverbial last straw that broke the camel's back, indeed that led me to come up with this book, was the experience I had recently working in a female prison. I came across a young inmate who was about the age of my daughter, 18 years old. She was in prison for drug-related offences (she committed theft to fund her addiction to heroin).

Doctors and other health professionals usually maintain an emotional distance from their patients as a defence mechanism to help them cope with the human misery and suffering they are exposed to on a regular basis. Though several years of work in the medical profession has conditioned me to withstand such emotional challenges, the fact that this young offender could easily have been my own daughter nearly broke my heart. If only to mollify my own conscience, I decided to come up with this book to educate the youth in particular and the general population at large concerning the risks inherent in the use of illicit drugs and alcohol.

The book, while touching on the possible cures available, will emphasise in the main *prevention*—for prevention, as the saying goes, is better than cure. Indeed, when it comes to the matter of substance abuse, the statement gains even more urgency.

Some tell me the problem of substance abuse has become a global problem of immense dimensions. The battle might well be described as long lost, to the extent that a book that seeks to counter it could be compared to dropping a single drop of red paint into a huge ocean with the aim of altering its colour. I have indeed no illusion as to the magnitude of the problem involved. Still, in my opinion, resignation in the face of the monstrous foe is not a way forward. If my effort leads even to a single individual refraining from trying or experimenting with the substances dealt with in this book, I will consider my goal as having been achieved.

Having said that by way of introduction, I shall now embark on the task I have set myself.

Loughborough, UK
October 2011

INTRODUCTION

FLEE, FLEE FOR YOUR LIFE!

H ave you ever been in acute danger and have had to flee for your life? I do remember some instances in my life when I found myself in such situations—situations that required me to escape quickly from impending danger.

On one such occasion, I was travelling on the back of an old, worn-out Bedford truck in my native Ghana, when all of a sudden, smoke billowed from the bonnet of the vehicle. Soon panic broke out among the travellers as everyone scrambled off the vehicle, which in the meantime the driver had managed to bring to a halt. Some, as they alighted, lost their balance and fell to the hard surface of the untarred road, only to be stepped upon by others jumping off the vehicle. Fortunately, apart from bruises, lacerations and superficial cuts, no one was seriously hurt.

I grew up in an African village under very tough circumstances. Like any child, I had to help my parents on the farm. When school was in session, I only needed to help out on Saturdays. During the school holidays I had to help with the farm work on almost every day apart from Sundays. The vegetation surrounding our little settlement was a tropical rain forest. The forest was populated by several kinds of wild and dangerous animals that could pose a threat to us. Though there were no elephants, tigers and lions in our area, there were still snakes, scorpions, wild bees, soldier ants, etc., which posed a constant threat. Whenever we left home to work on the farm, the fear of a possible confrontation with such potential enemies was always at the back of our minds.

The soldier ants—they could indeed be a menace! Army or soldier ants can be described as nomads that must migrate to find enough food to survive. They have carnivorous habits. Sometimes, as we worked on our farm, we would spot a large colony (a colony could be made up of up to one million ants!) heading in our direction. The sight of such an immense number of the aggressive insects could be pretty scary! Under such circumstances, there was no way of parleying with the impending danger. Instead, we took to our heels and escaped them.

Then there were the snakes! The tropical rain forest is home to several kinds of snakes—cobras, pythons, mambas, etc. Whenever we came into confrontation with them we took to our heels and ran for our lives—yes, ran away as quickly and as far as our legs could carry us.

Finally, I want to mention the wild bees. They could indeed cause havoc to their victims. Usually, the snakes, unless one accidentally stepped on them, would not bite. Instead, apparently also terrified by the presence of the intruding humans, they bolted as fast as they could. The situation was different with the wild bees. The moment they sighted the human intruder near their habitation, whether or not the two-footed trespasser had actively disturbed their habitation or not, they showed little mercy to the invader and went on the offensive. Even if the person fled the area, the aggressive creatures would not allow matters to rest there. Instead, they went in hot pursuit of the "offender". In many instances they succeeded in catching up with the fleeing human being. When that happened they stung mercilessly. The burning sensation resulting from their sting was excruciating to put it mildly.

In the same way that we fled for our lives when faced with danger and threats to our well-being, this book has, as its main goal, to warn readers, in particular the young among them, about the potential risks inherent in the use of the substances with the potential to addiction—alcohol, nicotine, cannabis, heroin, cocaine, etc.—and thus to urge them to flee from them.

Why the need to flee from the substances with the potential to addiction? The reasons are manifold. Allow me to dwell on a few of them. Among other things, we need to flee from them in order not to live to regret our actions—it could be too late, as in the case of a barely 21-year-old addict I came across in a prison in the UK. He was addicted not to one substance but several—alcohol, cannabis, crack cocaine, heroin and diazepam (more on diazepam later).

The medical staff had over the several weeks he was in prison made considerable efforts to help him cope with life in prison devoid of such substances, including prescribing medication that would help avert withdrawal symptoms (more on withdrawal symptoms later). Try as he did, he kept on struggling from the effects of his abstinence from the substances he was addicted to. One day, when I was alone with him, he looked me in the face and began:

"Doc, can you imagine what I would do to the person who first introduced me to drugs if I ever met him?"

"No, what would you do?"

"I will go for a gun and shoot him straight in the head!"

"No, no! You cannot do that!"

"He deserves nothing less after all the misery he has brought to my life! Tell me, Doc, what type of life is this? Is it worth living?"

The young man stated that his life was not worth living. Indeed, we need to flee from the substances of addiction because they have the power to take control of our minds, yes, enslave us, leading us to engage in behaviours that otherwise we would not dream of indulging in, including the following:

- Reckless and risky sexual behaviour that could eventually end in prostitution.
- Criminal behaviour—theft, assault, robbery—even armed robbery, burglary, fraud, etc.

Apart from the above, addiction to some of the substances to be considered in this book could also have an adverse effect on the following:

- **Our family**. Indeed, addiction to substances such as alcohol, cocaine and heroin, could lead to the breakdown of marriages and our relationship to other close family members as well as our close friends and associates.
- **Our business, property and savings**. As we spend considerable amounts of money daily to acquire some of the substances to be treated in this book, we could end up squandering our savings, selling our properties and assets—land, house, cars, etc.—having our houses repossessed as well as driving our otherwise thriving business into bankruptcy .
- **Our social standing**. The respect and esteem we hold in society could be ruined as our addiction to alcohol, cocaine, heroin, etc., forces us, otherwise decent and highly respected personalities of society, to engage in deeds unbecoming of our social standing.
- **Our health**. Worst of all, the substances under consideration could ruin our health, leading to the

acquisition of such serious infections and medical conditions such as hepatitis C, HIV/Aids, cirrhosis of the liver, deep vein thrombosis (DVT)—medical conditions that could lead to our untimely death.

PART ONE

GENERAL CONSIDERATIONS

Chapter 1

A GLOBAL PROBLEM OF
IMMENSE MAGNITUDE

The use of substances with the potential to addiction—alcohol, nicotine, cannabis, heroin, cocaine, etc.—is a global problem of huge dimensions, a problem that touches the lives of millions of people worldwide irrespective of colour, nationality, ideological leanings, socio-economic standing, religious inclinations, political affiliations, etc.

According to the WHO in 2008, 155 to 250 million people, or 3.5% to 5.7% of the world's population aged 15–64, used psychoactive substances (substances that affect the mind), such as cannabis, amphetamines, cocaine and heroin.

The BBC News Online for 1st January 2010 carried the following report:

Rising alcohol addiction costs could cripple the NHS
The cost of treating the growing number of people drinking heavily threatens to cripple NHS hospitals, warn experts.

If the trend continues the burden will be unsustainable, the Royal College of Physicians and NHS Confederation say.

With a quarter of England's population consuming hazardous amounts, alcohol addiction already costs the NHS more than £2.7 billion a year.

The situation is no better in my native Ghana. Though there are currently no reliable statistics available to determine the extent and trend of the magnitude of the problem, Ghana is currently reported to be seeing a devastating increase in the numbers of people who abuse drugs and consequently become addicted to it. Doctors and other health workers in the country say they are noticing a very disturbing trend of more and more pregnant women getting addicted to hard drugs like cocaine. They also report a steady rise in cases of foetal alcohol syndrome, where children are born displaying alcohol withdrawal symptoms because their mothers drank heavily during pregnancy.

Chapter 2

FACTORS THAT CAN LEAD TO SUBSTANCE ABUSE

❧

Having touched on the extent of the problem of drug abuse, I will move on to consider the factors that can lead an individual to abuse the substances in question.

The saying has it that "no one is born a criminal". Except in the instances when infants born to addicted mothers display drug-withdrawal symptoms (more of that later), it can also be said that no one is born a drug addict.

Though there is talk these days concerning studies that tend to associate the risk of becoming addicted to some of the substances of abuse around, in particular alcohol, with one's genes, the bottom line is that no one, irrespective of his or her genetic constitution, is forced to introduce the said substances into their bodies. Instead, one's path to addiction begins with a first *voluntary act.*

There is a saying in my mother tongue, *Twi*, "*Anya anto a, anya antua.*" Translated literally, it means, "If I do not buy, I do not pay!" Transposed into the current discussion, it could be modified as, "If I do not consume, I do not become addicted!"

In my opinion, any attempt at confronting the enormous challenges posed by the problem of substance addiction should aim at the factors that lead to addiction in the first place and the development of strategies to neutralise them.

What, then, are some of the factors generally recognised that lead to addiction? Though there are several of them, I shall concentrate on the following:

- family setting
- family breakdown
- societal influence
- peer pressure
- availability and affordability
- curiosity
- desire for performance enhancement, and finally
- as a way of getting over problems/stress.

FAMILY SETTING

Charity begins at home, so the old adage or saying goes. The saying is even truer when it comes to the issue of an individual's decision to try out or experiment with some of the substances of addiction.

While not implying that parents are always to be blamed if their children go on to become addicted to one substance or another, it is still true to say that children usually look to their parents for direction. They also tend to mimic or copy what they observe their parents or other adults around them are doing. When children observe family members smoking, drinking alcohol or abusing some of the substances under consideration, they may well be led to the conclusion that such practices are acceptable and lead them to do the same.

Indeed, it has been observed that children who grow up in a home in which one parent or both parents smoke, indulge in alcohol or any of the substances of abuse to be discussed in this book, are more likely than children whose parents do not partake of these substances to follow in their parents' footsteps and also abuse the substance involved.

FAMILY BREAKDOWN

Figures from the UK show that every third marriage breaks down at some time. The situation is no different from several other places under the sun. It is no secret that children usually suffer adversely from such ill-fated relationships. Among other things it could lead to poor parental control or supervision, which in turn could lead the children involved joining gangs or becoming associated with the wrong people, a situation that could make them vulnerable to and leave them exposed to drug users.

As a prison doctor working in various prisons in England, it has dawned on me through the taking of the medical history of inmates that a considerable proportion of those on drugs come from broken homes. My personal findings are supported by studies that have established that children who grow up in broken homes are more likely to go on to become addicted to substances of abuse than those who grow up in intact families.

SOCIETAL INFLUENCE

At the time I was growing up in my little village, Mpintimpi in the Eastern Region of Ghana, it was not uncommon for some of the adults in the community, even those I was not related to, to send me on errands to purchase certain items, including cigarettes and alcohol, from the few petty traders in the settlement (my parents did not themselves smoke). The practice of sending children on such errands continues to this day in Mpintimpi and several other communities in Ghana, especially those in the rural areas. I am certain the practice is not unique to Ghana but is true for other communities in the developing world.

Though this did not lead me to try my hand at them, some children sent on such errands may be tempted to consider the habits of the adults as normal, and be tempted to consume such substances also.

AFFORDABILITY AND AVAILABILITY

At our little village, alcohol was readily available—in the form of palm wine (an alcoholic drink obtained by tapping the sap of the palm tree) and *akpeteshie* (a highly potent drink obtained by distilling palm wine). Despite their availability, they were not affordable for everyone. (Residents were in the main poor peasant farmers.)

As a result of an affliction to my left ankle, I had to interrupt my elementary education for two years. In the course of time, a friend of my father's sought and obtained permission from him to permit me to assist him to sell his palm wine. This was done under the palm wine tapper's hut (a kind of village pub). Among my customers were those who, after drinking a calabash full of the alcoholic drink (a calabash could hold around 150ml), expressed the desire to consume more "calabashes" but were denied for the simple reason that they did not have cash on hand to pay for the additional drink. It may well have been that the person involved had even bought the first drink on credit after much pleading!

Some were denied even their first drink for the reason that they had on a previous visit drunk on credit promising to pay on the next visit, a promise they were unable to fulfil on the current visit. The Mpintimpi community was indeed an impoverished one, a community in which the average resident could rightly be compared to the proverbial poor church mouse. Thus, while the supply of the said alcoholic drinks was regular, the issue of affordability exercised some constraining effect on how much the average resident could consume.

Though palm wine was readily available in our village, this could not always be said of cigarettes. The few petty traders who sold them in the little settlement had to travel about 30 kilometres to Nkawkaw, the next big town, to purchase their wares for further sale to the villagers.

When a particular item was sold out, it was not immediately replaced. Instead the seller waited a while for the stock of most of the items on display to run down considerably or be sold out completely before embarking on the journey to Nkawkaw to replenish the stock. Another important factor that could delay the journey to replenish the stock was the fact that many customers bought on credit. Usually traders had to make several visits to them to retrieve what was owed them.

Even if the cigarettes were available, as in the case of alcoholic drinks, the issue of affordability served as a constraining factor for the average consumer.

As I just stated, the average citizen commanded a very meagre income. For most of the year, this was obtained through selling the small amounts of foodstuffs that such folk were able to harvest on their farms to the drivers and passengers of the few vehicles that stopped in the village on their way to and from the two main towns, Nkawkaw and Akim Oda.

It was only during the cocoa harvest season that they experienced a certain boost to their incomes resulting from the sale of the cocoa beans they harvested from their farms. Even then, many soon had to part with a considerable proportion of their earnings to pay off loans they had acquired from the few well-to-do's of the community during the "lean season", loans required to purchase clothes for their children, the wife or wives, as the case may be (it was a polygamous society), and for themselves.

These factors led to the practice that I will term "smoking in portions" among the few smokers of the little settlement. It involved the smoker smoking a portion of a stick of cigarette, then putting it out for a while only to light it after a while to smoke another fraction. The flame of the remaining piece was quenched only to be restarted another time. The ritual was repeated several times until the whole stick was consumed.

Still on the issue of affordability: though there are no figures to back my claim, it has generally been observed that in my native Ghana, children of the middle and upper classes are more likely than children of the lower income group to resort to substances of abuse such as cannabis and cocaine. The reason is not difficult to determine. For example, at the time I was growing up at Mpintimpi, my parents could not afford to give their children pocket money. Thus, even if one of us had wanted, for example, to smoke, that individual could hardly have afforded it. The situation was different for children of the middle and upper income groups living in the big towns and cities. Their parents could usually afford to give them pocket money, some of which could be spent on the said substances.

CURIOSITY

As I mentioned above, it was the practice of the few smokers at my childhood village to smoke cigarettes in "bits" or "instalments", for financial reasons. I recall a day when one of my peers and myself came across a piece of a half-smoked cigarette on the street. Apparently the smoker had inadvertently dropped it.

Children, children! Out of curiosity, my friend and I, after we picked it up, decided to light it and try it! On inhaling the smoke, I found it so awful and distasteful, I vowed never to repeat the experience. My friend made a similar decision. But what if I had given it a second, a third and perhaps a fourth try? That might well have been the beginning of my journey on the path of nicotine addiction. I will not advise anyone to imitate my example. Indeed, when it comes to substances with abuse potential, curiosity should have no place at all—never!

That brings to my mind the story I heard from a male nurse I met during my work as a prison doctor in England. I have no reason to doubt the truth behind his story. He told me that several years before our meeting, at the time when he was a teenager, he went to a disco with two other friends. As they approached the entrance to the disco, they were met by two men who were dealing in cannabis. They offered them some for free. According to him none of them had until then ever tried it. He rejected the offer. His two friends, on the other hand, could not resist the temptation and tried it. He went on to say that both friends went on to become addicted, not only to cannabis but also cocaine and heroin. According to his account, at the time he was telling the story, one of them had already died from a heroin overdose.

TO GET OVER PROBLEMS

I mentioned earlier on that as a result of an affliction to my left ankle, I had to interrupt my schooling for two years. At the beginning of my ordeal I was very sad and upset, not only because of the pain I had to bear, but also because of the sudden interruption to my educational career.

One day, I can no longer recall the exact circumstances, I had access to considerable amounts of palm wine. My young mind urged me to drink as much as I could, to get intoxicated, as way of expressing my sorrow, my disappointment at my fate. I wanted through my act to appeal for the pity of the outside world.

Though several years have elapsed since then, I still clearly recall that I did get really intoxicated, to the extent, for a while, that I could not stand on my feet! I felt horrible, really bad. At one stage the whole world appeared to be moving in circles before my eyes. It took several hours for me to recover from the terrible state. For the next few days, I felt the effect of my actions, as I continued to feel unwell. Just in the same way that the problem facing me led me to drink, many also take to the use of some of the substances under discussion to help them forget or get over the problems they may be facing.

PEER PRESSURE

A lady I interviewed the other day told me she was introduced to heroin by her lover, whom she adored and did not want to lose. She joined in the habit to, as it were, please him.

As the above example demonstrates, many, especially the young, may be lured into trying substances of abuse by their peers and/or lovers. Many teenagers and adolescents may be members of a gang. There is the tendency for members of the gang to do things in common. Because everyone is doing it, one is also tempted to do likewise, if only to please or to be accepted by other members.

One thing that we may lose sight of is that though we may try or indulge in such substances in a group, each individual will have to deal with the consequences of such joint action alone.

Let us assume we belong to a gang of five and all of us decide, for the first time, to try our hands at cannabis. We should bear in mind that we are made up of different building blocks, what the scientists refer to as genes. Indeed, the wonder of our being is that each one of us—apart from identical twins—are built of genes that are unique to ourselves. It may be the case that the genes of the other four members of our group, let us call them A, B, C and D, are better able to deal with the effect of cannabis on the body system with the result that they do not experience any further urge to retry it. On the other hand, the genes of yourself, Member E, are not able to deal with the effect of cannabis on your body, resulting in changes in your brain chemistry, leading you eventually to become addicted to it. In the end your habit leads you to commit crime—yes, even to shoplift—in order to support your addiction, a situation that in the end results in a prison sentence.

We note that though all gang members "experimented" with cannabis, only you would be paying for the consequences of that "experiment". Your friends may visit you in prison to show their sympathy and offer their solidarity, but at the end of their visit they are free to leave the jail whereas you will be left behind bars, to remain there until the end of your sentence.

DESIRE FOR PERFORMANCE ENHANCEMENT
Some, especially the youth, are lured into the use of some of the substances under consideration to help improve their academic performance. That this is wishful thinking will be touched upon at a later point in my discourse.

LOW SELF-ESTEEM
Some individuals have a low opinion of themselves, a situation that leads them to feel "worthless" and unwanted. This could lead them to, as it were, "give up" on life. A feeling of helplessness descends on them, leading them to become depressed. Some become withdrawn as they isolate themselves from daily activities such as going to work, or just going out for a walk or other physical activities. In such a situation an individual could become vulnerable and easily influenced by others to try out or resort to substances of abuse.

Chapter 3

COUNTERATTACK STRATEGIES
AGAINST A DEADLY FOE

H aving outlined the factors that lead to substance abuse, I want in this section to offer some thoughts, tips and suggestions as to how one could counter and overcome them.

FAMILY SETTING AND FAMILY BREAKDOWN
The insight I have gained working in several prisons in the UK, to which I referred earlier, is that many drug users grow up in broken homes. Usually after the breakdown of the marriage of their parents, they are left with only one parent, usually the mother. Whatever one's opinion of the matter is, it is generally recognised that a stable family where mother and father are present is the most suitable environment for the optimal development of a child.

Realising the positive effect a harmonious marriage has on the well-being of children, it can only be hoped that all stakeholders—married couples, policy makers, the church, other religious establishments, etc.—will do all that is within their means to strengthen not only the institution of marriage but also to prevent its breakdown.

If, despite all efforts to save it, a marriage breaks down, efforts should be undertaken, as far as possible, to ensure the children involved have as much access to both parents as possible, to facilitate their emotional well-being. Instead of considering their own personal interests, couples who have decided to go their separate ways should also give thought to the well-being of the children involved.

It is not uncommon that "battles" between couples engaged in long and bitter quarrels are fought over the heads of the children. The children eventually become emotionally torn between the two parents, a situation that does not augur well for their well-being, and that could eventually place them on the path of addiction.

SOCIETAL INFLUENCE

As I mentioned earlier, as a child I was sent on errands to purchase cigarettes for adults. It is not easy to break such cultural practices. Still, efforts should be undertaken to educate the adult population about the adverse effect such practices could have on children.

PEER PRESSURE

As a way of helping the young to overcome pressure from peers to try their hand at substances of abuse, some recommend they are trained in what has come to be known as "refusal skills". The sessions aim to equip youths with strategies they could apply when faced with temptation from other peers to join them in the use of some of the substances under discussion.

Among other things, such training involves role-play sessions. During such sessions, one of a group of young persons acts as the person having trouble refusing the pressure from his peers to try out a particular substance of abuse, while friends, relatives or acquaintances play the role of peers persuading him to experiment with the substance in question.

GETTING OVER PROBLEMS

I narrated earlier how I once got drunk as a result of a challenge I was facing. Did my problem go away as a result of it? Of course not. Just in the same way that I sought in vain to drink myself out of my problem, many are led into alcoholism and the abuse of other substances in the vain hope that these might help them overcome the problems, burdens and stressful situations confronting them.

I urge the reader facing life's challenges, who may be contemplating such a move, to learn from my experience and desist from treading a similar path. There certainly are more suitable ways of dealing with the problems and challenges that may come our way in life than to seek refuge in a chemical substance. At best such substances may provide only temporary relief. What is more likely to happen is that they could set one on the path of addiction.

PERFORMANCE ENHANCEMENT

That the use of any substance could lead one to improve one's academic performance is born out of illusion.

My own personal experience tells me that we can only achieve our set goals in life through hard work, determination, perseverance in the face of seemingly insurmountable odds, singleness of purpose, etc. I do not want to blow my trumpet before the whole world. My schoolmates will surely bear witness to the fact that I was one of the bright pupils in our year group. Still, I did not take risks when it came to academic work.

During my secondary school days in Ghana, the practice of "mining", whereby a student stayed awake deep into the night to revise for an impending examination, was quite popular among students, especially those in boarding schools. How many times did I and other study mates gather together, deep into the night, to study for an impending examination!

I thought the need to go "mining" would end with the completion of my secondary school education. I had reason to think otherwise during my time at medical school. Indeed, I soon realised that at medical school the practice of "mining" was not only necessary, but needed to be undertaken even more frequently than was the case in secondary school. As a matter of fact, at the end of the day it was hard work and dedication to my books that led to success and not the result of resorting to any substance of abuse.

So, dear young reader, if you are contemplating the use of substances such as ecstasy, amphetamine, cannabis, etc., in the hope that it will boost your academic performance, you would do well to discard that thought and instead get down to serious academic work to achieve your goal.

LOW SELF-ESTEEM
This book is not intended to be a lecture on how one can overcome one's low self-esteem. Also, I do not claim to be an expert in that sphere. I think what is needed is for parents to acknowledge the achievements of their children, however insignificant we might consider those achievements to be. That could positively influence their outlook and encourage them to strive hard to achieve even better outcomes in whatever they set out to do.

PART TWO

TERMINOLOGIES DEFINED

Chapter 4

LATIN MADE EASY

B efore I look closely at some of the substances of addiction around, I first want to explain some of the terms associated with the topic. To prevent my narration from turning into a boring monologue, I will refer, in several instances, to down-to-earth illustrations, for the most part dating back to my childhood and boyhood days at Mpintimpi.

SUBSTANCE ABUSE
Though there is no universally accepted definition of substance abuse, the term is generally used to describe the excessive use of a substance, any physical matter, especially alcohol, a drug or other chemical, leading to effects that are harmful or detrimental to the individual's physical and mental health, or the welfare of others. Although there are several potential substances of abuse, this book will limit itself to alcohol, nicotine (found in cigarette smoke), cannabis (marijuana), ecstasy, amphetamine, diazepam (commonly known as valium), solvents, cocaine and heroin.

POLYSUBSTANCE ABUSE
The term is defined as the abuse of more than one substances of addiction, examples of which have just been listed. For example,

an inmate in a prison in England where I worked as a doctor admitted to using the following substances on a daily basis:

- Alcohol: 6 to 8 cans of beer plus some bottles of wine
- Heroin: about £80 worth
- Crack cocaine: about £80 worth
- Diazepam: 30mg daily
- Cannabis: about £10 worth.

His information was confirmed by the result of the test conducted on his urine, which turned out positive for all the above-named substances apart from alcohol (alcohol cannot be detected in urine).

Prior to my work as a prison doctor, it was not clear to me how widespread the problem was among drug users. I am now better informed. Indeed, among drug users, especially the young among them, hardly anyone abuses only a single substance. Instead, the general trend is for individuals to be addicted to two, three and—as the above example shows—even more substances at the same time.

Polysubstance abusers usually develop a "drug of choice", which is the drug they prefer to abuse, with the other drugs serving as a fallback when the drug of choice is not available. Although drug abuse in general leads to criminal activity, poly-drug abusers are more likely to resort to criminal activity to fund their habit compared to those who are addicted to only one substance.

GATEWAY DRUG

In normal life one cannot all of a sudden become a medical doctor, a pilot or a lawyer. Instead, one has first to go to primary school, then secondary school, and finally to other institutions of higher learning such as teacher training colleges, polytechnics, universities, etc.

A similar pattern can be observed in the matter of substance misuse. Indeed, hardly anyone begins his/her journey of addiction with a "hard" drug such as heroin or cocaine. Instead, such individuals usually start their "drug career" with so-called "soft" substances such as alcohol, cigarettes and cannabis. A teenager, for example, may first experiment with cigarettes and/or alcohol. In time, they may be tempted to try their hand at cannabis. In the end that individual could end up abusing more potent substances such as heroin or cocaine, or both.

Substances such as alcohol, nicotine (cigarettes) and cannabis, the habitual use of which could lead one to the abuse of more harmful substances such as cocaine and heroin, are referred to as *gateway drugs*.

ADDICTION

Each one of us is endowed with will power, the will to do whatever we want to do at any particular time. For example, no one forced me to get up early and sit in front of my laptop to write this book. In the same way, you are reading these lines out of your own free will.

Even when it comes to taking in food that sustains us, strictly speaking it can still be described as a voluntary act, for indeed no one can force us to eat. You may think of several other examples from daily life.

When one tries the substances of addiction under consideration, initially, one is usually able to decide when to consume the substance involved and when to abstain from it for a while.

Should an individual continue to use a substance with a potential to addiction on a regular basis, a stage is usually reached when the person involved loses control over the ability

Robert Peprah-Gyamfi

to decide when and where to consume the said substance. At that stage that individual could be said to have become addicted to the substance in question.

What then is addiction? The *Oxford English Dictionary* defines it as "the state of being enslaved to a habit or a practice"! The word *enslaved*, in turn, is defined as a state whereby an individual has lost the freedom of choice or action to someone else. At that stage the affected individual would be considered wholly under the domination of the substance involved, and a master–bondservant relationship would have developed—the human addict being as it were the bondservant to the substance involved.

Let us pause a while to reflect on the matter. The human being, the most intelligent being in the universe, has become a bondservant to a chemical substance such as heroin or cocaine!

In normal life, a slave cannot on his/her own bidding get up one day and free him/herself from the realm of authority of the master. In the same way, a person addicted to a particular substance cannot get up one day and bid farewell to the stuff involved. The individual who dares do so must reckon with what is termed withdrawal symptoms, which in some instances, alcohol being a typical example, could even lead to the death of the affected person.

There are two aspects of addiction: psychological and physical addiction.

Psychological addiction: The *mind* of a person addicted to a particular substance has an irresistible or uncontrollable craving or longing for the substance involved. Such a person may go to great lengths to acquire the substance involved. To achieve that goal, the individual may resort to lying, stealing, spending excessive amounts of time and money, etc. Although aware of the negative consequences of their behaviour, a person psychologically addicted to a substance will still crave for the substance involved.

Physical addiction, tolerance and drug withdrawal: I shall use a story dating back to my boyhood days to help explain the concept of physical addiction and the related terminology, tolerance.

I mentioned earlier that as a result of an affliction to my left ankle I ended up selling palm wine instead of attending school. In the course of time I became aware of two types of drinkers. There were those whose behaviour, even after consuming a single calabash full of the palm wine, led to the conclusion that they were beginning to "lose control". Then there was the second group of drinkers, individuals who would consume one, then two, then three and even more calabashes full of the alcoholic drink without displaying the least signs of intoxication. My young mind could only wonder at the "resilience" of such group of drinkers, drinkers who gained the Twi accolade "*oweeye!*"— super drinkers! Now I am better informed—the "*oweeye*" or super drinker had developed *tolerance* to alcohol whereas the first group had not.

Indeed, one of the characteristics of the substances of abuse is that continual use can lead the body to become increasingly able to withstand the effects of the substance. Ultimately one has to introduce larger amounts of the substance in question in order to achieve the desired effect. At that stage the body is said to have developed a tolerance to the substance in question.

I got another sense of how individuals could become tolerant to chemical substances during my work as a prison doctor in England. I shall use the substance diazepam (more about diazepam later) as an example. A textbook of medicine or pharmacology would likely state that the maximum daily dose of diazepam is 30 milligrams (mgs) spread over the day, usually 10mgs three times daily. As a prison doctor, I was shocked to hear inmates admit to the size of the daily dose of the said substance they were taking prior to being sent to prison. Some reported taking as much as 50, 100 and more milligrams of the said substances on a daily basis, in some cases as a single dose! Such a high dose of diazepam could lead to serious trouble, even the death of the individual whose body is not used to it.

Still another story from my days at Mpintimpi might shed some light on the issue of physical addiction and drug withdrawal. There used to be a prominent personality, a good friend of father's, living in a small village bordering on our own. He was well known by all for his love of alcohol, not for the least potent among them, but rather for the highly potent *akpeteshie*.

In the course of time, rumours began to circulate in the little settlement to the effect that the individual concerned had been to the doctors at the hospital at Nkawkaw, about 30 kilometres away, to seek help for a medical condition not related to his alcohol problem. The rumours went on to state that, on his discharge from hospital, the doctors advised him against stopping drinking because the moment he did so, he would *die!* The individual took the advice of the doctors, as it were, as a licence to continue drinking!

Laymen in the field of medicine that we, the simple residents of the village, were, how could anyone challenge the advice that was purported to have come from the medical experts?! Still, that assertion would not leave my young mind to rest. I really found it strange that the doctors would, as it were, *encourage* someone to keep on drinking instead of advising against it.

Now, with my present knowledge, and my familiarity with the circumstances prevailing in the little village at that time, I am beginning to figure out what could have led the doctors to give that advice (if indeed they really did so). The doctors might have taken into consideration the issue of physical dependence and drug-withdrawal symptoms. What then is physical dependence?

Physical dependence on a substance develops when the body has become dependent on the substance to the extent that an abrupt cessation of its use leads to untoward reactions known as withdrawal symptoms.

Now, let me return to the case of our compatriot. The doctors, aware that he was physically addicted to alcohol, might have concluded that advising him to continue with his habit was the lesser of two evils compared to the potentially life-threatening withdrawal symptoms that could result from abstinence from alcohol.

It must be said that not everyone who stops drinking experiences withdrawal symptoms, but most people who have been drinking frequently for a long period of time, or who have been drinking heavily, will experience some form of withdrawal symptoms if they stop drinking suddenly.

RELAPSE

Have you come across someone who told you he/she has conquered his/her addiction to alcohol, cannabis, cigarettes, cocaine, heroin, etc., only to meet the same individual just a few days later engaged in the very habit he/she was supposed to have overcome?

"But you told me you have conquered your dependence on substance A!" you confront him/her.

"Well, the soul is willing but the body is weak; I really did all I could to suppress the temptation, but in the end I had to succumb to it!" might be the reply.

As I pointed out earlier on, I have been working as a doctor in various prisons in the UK. I also mentioned that a good proportion of the inmates are poly-drug users, addicted to more than one substance at the same time. Usually during their stay in prison they are gradually weaned off the particular substance or substances of addiction involved. After serving their various prison terms, and as they are about to be released, the following conversation between me and some of them might take place:

"Doc, I am going home tomorrow."

"That's good news. I hope this is going to be your last time behind bars."

"Sure, sure! Enough is enough. This has been my third time in prison. This time I am definitely going to stay 'clean!' and away from crime!"

"All the best, my friend, all the best!"

I have on a few instances in this book referred to the saying "the soul is willing, but the flesh is weak!" When it comes to the substances of addiction, the saying is even truer. Indeed, how many times has a person addicted to a particular substance become "clean" of the substance in question only to relapse, or return to the use of the substance in question. That partly if not fully accounts for the return of several of the inmates I met in prison, back behind bars after a few months, if not weeks or even days after they had sworn never to return to prison.

When I found such inmates yet again before me I would usually begin:

"What are you doing here?"

"I got myself into trouble again, Doc!"

"But you swore never to return!"

"Easier said than done, Doc, easier said than done!"

"What happened?"

"Shoplifting!"

"What?"

"Men's aftershave! I needed money for 'stuff!'"—was a typical reply.

DETOXIFICATION

In a previous section I touched on drug-withdrawal symptoms. As I have stressed on several occasions in this book, it is not usually possible for individuals, once they have become addicted to a substance of abuse, to abruptly stop using the substance in question. In order to help an addicted person determined to do so achieve the set goal, the individual involved has to undergo detoxification.

The term *detoxification* is derived from the word *toxin* which stands for any poisonous substance that is capable of causing disease when introduced into the body. The process of detoxification aims thus to free the body system from the "poison", the substance of addiction in question. In the detoxification process a person addicted to a substance is deprived of the substance involved until such time that the bloodstream is "detoxed" or freed of the substance in question. During the process of detoxification, the individual involved is prescribed medication that either prevents the expected withdrawal reaction from taking place or lessens its impact on the body. The process is usually medically supervised, either by a doctor, a nurse or medical personnel specially trained for the purpose.

THE BRAIN REWARD SYSTEM

The question that one may ask is: being aware of the harmful effects of the substances of abuse under discussion on the body, why are they still consumed? Earlier on we noted some of the factors that can lead one to try such substances.

Whereas the factors mentioned above—peer pressure, curiosity, availability, affordability, etc.—could lead one to the first voluntary act of the consumption of the substance in question, soon, however, another factor, namely the influence of the brain reward system, could enter into the equation to complicate matters.

Through research, it has been established that specific areas of the brain control specific functions of the body such as hearing, seeing, limb movement, etc. The part of the brain associated with emotions and motivations, particularly those related to survival, such as fear and anger, is known as the limbic system.

The limbic system is also involved in pleasurable activities such as eating, drinking and sex. Most drugs of abuse activate the reward circuit in the brain, producing in the process pleasurable feelings to the drug user. And, because the feelings are pleasurable, the user is inclined to want to repeat the same action, that is consume the same drug in order to experience the same pleasure felt during the previous drug use.

The brain is divided into several parts. I have just referred to the limbic system. Another part of the brain is known as the cortex. The cortex is responsible among other things for thinking and reasoning. It has been established that the limbic system upon which the substances of addiction act is capable of overriding the actions of the cortex, which, as we have just learnt, is responsible for reasoning and thinking. The implication is that in the end, a person addicted to a substance could lose control of his/her addictive behaviour.

PART THREE

WEAPONS OF A DREADFUL ENEMY

Chapter 5

NICOTINE:
The addiction that comes in a smoke

CHEMISTRY OF NICOTINE

N icotine, which is contained in the smoke of a cigarette, is represented by the chemical formula $C_{10}H_{14}N_2$.

The chemical nicotine is produced in the roots of the tobacco plant and then carried to the leaves, where it is stored. When one smokes a cigarette, the individual inhales nicotine into his or her lungs with the tobacco smoke. Nicotine is not the only substance contained in the smoke of cigarettes; there are instead about 4,000 other chemicals involved. Among the 4,000 chemicals, more than 40 are known to cause cancer.

Nicotine is highly addictive. In other words, once one has had a taste of it, one soon becomes physically and psychologically dependent on it. When smoked, nicotine activates the reward system in the brain, leading the individual to feel a sense of pleasure. It is this effect of nicotine on the body that can over a time lead to addiction.

HEALTH PROBLEMS CAUSED BY SMOKING
Cigarette smoking is a health risk. There are short- as well as long-term adverse or harmful effects to the body of smoking.

SHORT-TERM EFFECTS
Respiratory system: The smoke inhaled from cigarettes causes the lung to contract or reduce its volume. This can lead to breathing problems, especially in the person already suffering from diseases affecting the lungs, such as asthma.

Digestive system: It could lead to nausea (feel like vomiting), heartburn, dry mouth, diarrhoea, indigestion.

Heart and circulatory system: It can cause the heart to beat faster than expected and also lead to increased blood pressure. Besides that, nicotine could lead to a reduction in the flow of blood to the heart and also an increase in the formation of blood clots.

Muscles: It could lead to muscles shaking (tremor) and also pain.

Central nervous system (CNS): Among other things smoking can lead to headaches, dizziness and sleep disturbance.

Effect on pregnancy: Pregnant women who smoke run an increased risk of having stillborn babies (babies who are born already dead) or premature infants (babies born before term) or infants with birth weights lower than expected for an average baby.

LONG-TERM EFFECTS

Cancer: As I stated above, apart from nicotine, cigarette smoke contains several cancer-causing substances. Apart from being the major cause of lung cancer, smoking is also associated with several other types of cancers. These include cancers of the larynx (the portion of the breathing, or respiratory tract containing the vocal cords that produce vocal sound), oesophagus (gullet), bladder, kidney, pancreas (an organ situated behind the stomach, which secretes insulin and digestive enzymes), stomach and the womb.

Respiratory system:
- **Chronic bronchitis:** Smoking is also the major cause of bronchitis (swelling of the airways leading to the lungs), both acute and chronic.
- **Emphysema:** (A condition in which the air sacs of the lungs are damaged and enlarged, causing breathlessness.)
- **Chronic infections**: Smoking is also associated with an increased incidence of respiratory infections.

Heart and circulatory diseases: Cigarette smoking is associated with heart disease and strokes. (A stroke is caused by the interruption of the blood supply to the brain, usually because a blood vessel bursts or is blocked by a clot. This cuts off the supply of oxygen and nutrients, causing damage to the brain tissue.)

Smoking, ultimately, can lead to the medical condition known as peripheral vascular disease (PVD). In this condition the arteries that supply the limbs with blood keep getting narrower. This leads to poor circulation of blood to the affected parts of the body. PVD, in its extreme form, can lead to the amputation, or removal, of the affected limb.

TOBACCO CHEWING, CIGAR AND PIPE SMOKING
Before I leave the area of smoking, I want to devote a few lines to cigar and pipe smoking, as well as the habit of tobacco chewing. The practice can, in the end, also lead to nicotine addiction.

Although cigar and pipe smokers have lower death rates compared to cigarette smokers, they are still susceptible to various kinds on cancers, especially those affecting the mouth, the larynx and the oesophagus.

NICOTINE-WITHDDRAWAL SYMPTOMS
A person addicted to nicotine will experience withdrawal reactions if he or she abruptly or suddenly stops smoking. Following are some of the nicotine-withdrawal symptoms:

- **Anger and anxiety**. There is a saying that a hungry man is an angry man. This could also be said of a smoker deprived of cigarettes. Such an individual could become irritable, nervous and explode in anger at the slightest provocation. So beware of your relative, friend or colleague who might be attempting to quit the habit. The least provocation could lead to an outburst of anger in such individuals!
- **Increased appetite and hunger**. Smokers attempting to break their habit report an increased appetite and hunger in the early stages. The other day one of my patients told me she was reluctant to give up her habit for fear it would lead to her putting on extra weight. That had happened to an acquaintance of hers and she did not want to suffer a similar fate. I cannot tell whether my acquaintance was making excuses to explain her inability to give up her habit. In any case, it has been observed that those who give up smoking, at least in the short term, experience an increased craving for food. If uncontrolled, this could

indeed lead to an increase in body weight. While aware of the health risks posed by obesity (being overweight), the moderate increase in weight that could result from the cessation of smoking might be regarded as the lesser of two evils given the health risks posed by smoking.

- **Depression.** As we saw earlier on, smoking, if only in the short term, confers (bestows) to the smoker a certain degree of good feeling. Stopping the habit could, at least in the short term, have the opposite effect of making the affected person feel depressed.

Other symptoms of nicotine withdrawal are: coughing, sleep disturbance, headaches, poor concentration and tiredness.

Chapter 6

CANNABIS:
The most commonly abused
substance worldwide

A lso known as marijuana, cannabis is a mixture of the dried and shredded leaves, stems, seeds, and flowers of the plant known by its botanical name of *cannabis sativa*. It is the world's most commonly used substance of addiction. It is known by several different names, depending on the country involved.

In my native Ghana, the terms include "Indian hemp", "wee", "ntampi". Some other "international" names for cannabis are: "pot", "grass", "herb", "weed", "Mary Jane", "reefer", "skunk", "boom", "gangster", "kif", "chronic", and "ganja".

Cannabis is used in many ways. The most common method is smoking loose cannabis rolled into a cigarette called a "joint" or "nail". Sometimes cannabis is smoked through a water pipe called a "bong". Others smoke "blunts"—cigars hollowed out and filled with the drug. Cannabis can also be brewed into tea or mixed in baked products (cookies or brownies).

Although it contains at least 400 different chemicals, the main psychoactive or mind-altering ingredient of the plant is delta-9-tetrahydrocannabinol or THC for short. The strength or potency of cannabis is indeed related to (dependent on) the amount of

THC it contains. Put in other words, the more the concentration of THC in cannabis, the stronger its effects on its user.

The active ingredient, THC, acts on receptors on nerve cells known as cannabinoid receptors. In so doing they are able to influence the activity of those cells. Some brain areas have many cannabinoid receptors, but other areas of the brain have few or none at all. Many cannabinoid receptors are found in the parts of the brain that influence pleasure, memory, thought and concentration. The influence of THC on cannabinoid receptors leads to the creation of a good feeling or "high" in the consumer. It is this effect that may drive the user to consume (smoke) cannabis again and again, to recreate that experience, a situation that in the end could lead to addiction.

EFFECTS OF CANNABIS ON THE BODY

The effects of smoking cannabis are generally felt within a few minutes and reaches a climax in 10 to 30minutes. It can affect the body in various ways.

Effects on the brain: Cannabis can adversely affect brain function and hamper the individual in his or her ability to perform complex or difficult assignments. This could, for example, prevent the affected person from achieving good grades in school and in so doing prevent him or her from pursuing academic goals that demand high concentration.

Cannabis can also affect memory, judgment and decision making. Under the influence of cannabis, the individual is inclined to reckless and risky behaviour, causing one to do things that one would otherwise not consider doing under normal circumstances. These may include risky sexual behaviour, which in turn could expose the individual to the risk of contracting or acquiring sexually transmitted diseases such as HIV/AIDS;

risky behaviour might also include dangerous driving, speeding, dangerous overtaking, etc.

It has also been observed that early use of cannabis may increase the risk of the development of psychosis in later life. A severe mental disorder might develop in which there is a loss of contact with reality; including false ideas about what is happening (delusions) and seeing or hearing things that aren't there (hallucinations).

Effects on the respiratory system: Cannabis smokers are more inclined to catch respiratory diseases. These include colds, coughs, bronchitis, lung infection asthma, etc. The risk of lung cancer is also increased in cannabis smokers.

Effect on the immune system: There is evidence that cannabis may limit the ability of the immune system to fight infection and disease.

Effect on onset of puberty: Regular use of cannabis can delay the onset of puberty in young men. For women, regular use may disrupt normal monthly menstrual cycles.

Effect on pregnancy: When pregnant women use cannabis, they run the risk of giving birth to babies with low birth weights. Such babies are more likely than others to develop health problems.

CANNABIS-WITHDRAWAL SYMPTOMS
Deprived of cannabis, those addicted to it may experience withdrawal symptoms. The symptoms usually set in between the second and tenth day of quitting and can last for up to a month in some people.

The most common cannabis-withdrawal symptoms are:

- **Low grade anxiety**.
- **Insomnia** (sleeplessness or inability to sleep). This could be particularly severe in the initial stages.
- **Change of appetite and weight loss**. Many who attempt to give up smoking cannabis complain of loss of appetite. This could be because many cannabis smokers find the need to smoke before they eat. After quitting the habit, at least in the initial stages, they lose the desire to eat. Lack of appetite in turn could lead to weight loss. The above symptoms could last for several days to a few weeks.

Chapter 7

HALLUCINOGEN:
Drugs that lead users to see, feel or sense things that are not there!

A lso known as psychedelic drugs, hallucinogens are chemicals that are capable of the following: affecting the way one thinks, influencing the way the individual perceives the physical world as well as the way the he or she senses the passing of time.

The substances involved are capable of changing the mood or state of mind of the user and lead the affected person to behave in a strange manner. For example, they can lead the user to experience hallucinations. Hallucination is a situation where someone experiences an effect that does not exist in reality. Hallucinations may take several forms. In acoustic hallucination, the individual hears voices that do not exist; in visual hallucination the affected person sees objects that are not there; in olfactory hallucination, the person involved can scent smells that no one else around can smell.

For many individuals under the influence of hallucinogens, the separation between the individual and the environment disappears, leading to a sense of oneness or holiness. The effects, sometimes referred to as a "good trip", can last from an hour to a few days. Such "good trips" could alternate with "bad trips" full of frightening images, monsters, and paranoid thoughts. The term *paranoid* is derived from "paranoia". Paranoia is an unfounded or exaggerated distrust of others. Paranoid individuals constantly suspect the motives of those around them, and believe that certain individuals, or people in general, are "out to get them". Flashbacks or unexpected reappearances of the effects can occur months later.

EXAMPLES OF HALLUCINOGEN DRUGS

ECSTASY
Ecstasy is a synthetic hallucinogen drug. It is represented by a long chemical formula: 3-4 methylenedioxymethamphetamine or MDMA.

It is known by several street names. These include the following: Adam, Xtc, X, Hug, Go, Hug Drug, Beans and Love Drug.

Ecstasy is usually produced in a tablet form. This is usually swallowed, though it can also be crushed and snorted, injected, or used in the form of a suppository.

The drug is known for its energising effect. Its popularity grew out of its reputation for producing high energy that could enable its users to stand on their feet and dance for hours without becoming exhausted.

Effects on the mind
The effect of ecstasy on the mind includes the following: confusion, anxiety, depression as well as sleep disturbance.

Effects on the body
The effects of ecstasy use on the body are varied and can last for weeks. These include muscle tension, involuntary teeth

clenching, nausea, blurred vision, sweating, chills, increased heart rate and blood pressure (which could worsen an already existing heart condition).

In the long term, ecstasy users face the risk of liver damage.

Esctasy-withdrawal symptoms
Withdrawal symptoms in ecstasy users include: fatigue or tiredness, loss of appetite, feelings of depression as well as difficulty concentrating.

AMPHETAMINE
Amphetamines (a lpha - m ethyl - ph en et hyl amine), are highly addictive central nervous system stimulants (an agent, especially a chemical agent that leads to a short-term increase in bodily activity).

As with other substances of abuse, amphetamine is known by several street names, including bennies, glass, crystal, crank, pep pills, and uppers.

Street amphetamine is sold as crystals, chunks, and fine to coarse powders or in capsules or tablets of various sizes and colours.

The injectable form of amphetamine, methamphetamine, also known as "speed", is a popular version of the drug. Users report a more rapid and intense "high" through that form of administration than when the drug is swallowed. Amphetamine can also be snorted, smoked, or ingested orally.

Short-term effects
Physical: At low doses physical effects include loss of appetite, rapid breathing, rapid heartbeat, raised blood pressure and dilated pupils. Larger doses may produce fever, sweating, headache, blurred vision, and dizziness. Very high doses may cause very rapid or irregular heartbeat, tremors, loss of coordination,

and collapse. Deaths have been reported as a direct result of amphetamine use or indirectly as a result of burst blood vessels in the brain, heart failure, or very high fever.

Psychological: The short-term effect on the mind includes a feeling of well-being and great alertness and energy. With increased doses, users may become talkative, restless, and excited, and may feel a sense of power and superiority. They may also behave in a bizarre, repetitive fashion. Many become hostile and aggressive.

Long-term effects
Because amphetamines specifically suppress appetite, chronic heavy users generally fail to eat properly and thus develop various illnesses related to malnutrition. Users may also be more prone to illness because they are generally run down, lacking in sleep, and live in an unhealthy environment.

Chronic heavy users may in the end develop amphetamine psychosis, though the symptoms usually disappear within a few days or weeks after drug use is stopped.

Amphetamine-withdrawal symptoms
The most common withdrawal symptoms among heavy amphetamine users are fatigue, long but troubled sleep, irritability, intense hunger, and moderate to severe depression, which may lead to suicidal behaviour.

Chapter 8

INHALANTS:
Vapours that affect the mind

Inhalants are breathable chemical vapours that can influence the mind of their users. They include gases, solvents and nitrites.

When inhaled, the substances initially lead to stimulation and loss of inhibition. Loss of inhibition could lead users among other things to engage in carefree and reckless behaviour. The initial feeling of excitement and happiness may be followed later by a feeling of low mood or depression.

Inhalants could initially lead to the following: headache, nausea, vomiting and slurred speech.

Prolonged use could lead to anaemia or blood shortage as well as damage to the brain, bone marrow and the kidneys.

Chapter 9

HEROIN:
Injections that bring misery instead of cure

A lso known as diacetylmorphine, heroin is represented by the chemical formula $C_{17}H_{17}NO\ (C_2H_3O_2)_2$. It is a highly addictive drug derived from morphine, which is obtained from the opium poppy. In its purest form it is a white, odourless, bitter crystalline compound. In its impure form it can be brown in colour.

Heroin is known by various street names. These include smack, horse, mud, brown sugar, goods, H and junk. Street heroin is often cut or mixed with other substances such as glucose or talcum powder. The practice in itself may be dangerous and make it difficult for the user to know the exact dose being taken. Although heroin is most commonly injected it is often also smoked. Whether injected or smoked, heroin will begin to affect the body's central nervous system almost immediately after it is used.

The practice of injecting heroin into the body can itself lead to several problems. Among other things it can lead to infection of the injected sites, which in turn could lead to serious complications.

Apart from the danger of infection resulting directly from the use of unclean needles, infection could also result from the practice of sharing needles and other equipment, a common practice among addicts.

Apart from infection that directly affects the injection sites, injecting could lead to infection in remote sites such as endocarditis (an infection of the lining of the heart chambers and heart valves that is caused by bacteria, fungi, or other infectious substances), HIV/AIDS, hepatitis (disease of the liver, caused by a virus or a toxin and characterised by jaundice, liver enlargement, and fever).

Injection can also lead to damage of the veins. In time addicts find it difficult to inject into the veins of the arms. In their desperation to find veins to inject into, some addicts resort to the large veins of the groin and the neck!

Many a trained doctor would tell you they are reluctant to inject into such major veins of the body due to complications that can be severe and life-threatening. If even doctors are reluctant to tamper with such veins, how reckless and much more dangerous it is for untrained individuals who dare to do so!

That, however, is an indication of the extent to which many a heroin addict will go! Spurred on by their extreme craving for the substance, not a few of them take the risk upon themselves and inject heroin into the great veins of the groin and the neck, closing their eyes to possible complications such as—infection, ruptured veins, blood clot formation, which in turn could travel from the point of formation to distant sites to block some of the great veins leading from the heart into the lungs, which in turn could lead to the death of the affected person.

EFFECT OF HEROIN ON THE BODY

Short-term effects: Shortly after its introduction into the body, a feeling of euphoria or great happiness and well-being is experienced by the user. The initial rush is followed by a state that could alternate between wakefulness and drowsiness.

Heroin suppresses the central nervous system including the area of the brain that controls breathing, also known as the respiratory centre. Suppression of the respiratory centre could lead to a slowing down of the rate of respiration. In high doses of heroin, the suppression of the breathing centre could be so intense or forceful, it could lead to complete cessation of breathing and ultimately the death of the affected person.

Other short-term effects of the use of heroin include nausea, vomiting, loss of appetite and pain relief (both physical and mental pain).

Long-term effects: Repeated and chronic heroin users who fail to use sterile techniques or share equipment may be subjected to the following long-term adverse effects:

- infection of the heart lining and valves
- liver disease—especially hepatitis C infections
- chronic infection of the respiratory system
- skin infections and abscesses, usually resulting from the injection sites
- kidney disease.

OTHER EFFECTS OF HEROIN USE
On pregnancy: Using heroin when one is pregnant can lead to several problems. Among other things, it could result in:

- **Premature birth**. (If a baby is born before 37 weeks from the time of conception to the time of birth it is considered premature.)
- **Stillbirth**. (An infant that shows no signs of life after birth.)

- **Sudden death syndrome** of the resulting birth. (A situation whereby an infant or a toddler dies suddenly without any established cause.)

On children born to addicts: Even if the children survive in the womb of their mothers, such children display low birth weights. In other words, children born to heroin addicts are smaller than children of mothers who do not have such a problem.

Withdrawal symptoms in the newborn: During the time they are developing in the wombs of their mothers, babies of drug addicts absorb the drug in question from the mother's bloodstream into their own blood system. After birth, that stops. The abrupt deprivation of the substance from the body system of the baby leads to the same withdrawal symptoms described above for the adult addict.

HEROIN-WITHDRAWAL SYMPTOMS
If a person addicted to heroin is suddenly deprived of the substance, it could lead to the following withdrawal symptoms.

Early symptoms:
- Agitation
- Anxiety
- Muscle aches
- Insomnia
- Runny nose
- Sweating
- Yawning

Late symptoms:
- Abdominal cramping
- Diarrhoea (running stomach)
- Dilated pupils
- Goose bumps
- Nausea
- Vomiting

Chapter 10

COCAINE:
First the "high" then the awful "crash"!

Cocaine is a white crystalline powder. It is obtained from the leaves of the coca plant, which grows in South America. Like the other substances of addiction already treated, cocaine is known by several names. These include coke, dust, snow, flake, the lady, etc.

It can be injected, smoked, sniffed, or snorted. Its effects can last from 20 minutes to several hours, depending on the dosage of cocaine taken, its purity, and method of administration.

Cocaine is a powerful stimulant, leading temporarily to an increase in the activity of the body, in particular the central nervous system. Initially it creates a strong sense of happiness and well-being in the user leading them generally to feel incapable of being "conquered" or overcome. They also feel especially alert and carefree.

This initial feeling of being as it were "on top of the world" is usually followed by agitation, depression, anxiety, paranoia and decreased appetite.

HARMFUL EFFECTS ON THE BODY

Short–term effects: The short-term risk posed by cocaine to the user is the danger of cardiac arrest (heart stoppage), which in turn could lead to cessation of breathing and death. The user could also experience epileptic fits or seizures.

Other short-term effects include: sleep disturbance, loss of appetite, blurred vision, sweating and hallucination.

Long-term effects: The long-term effects of cocaine use may include extreme agitation, violent mood swings and depression. Small ulcers or wounds may also form on the skin inside the nose and also on the walls separating the two chambers of the nose of users who snort or suck the substance forcefully through the nose. In time it leads to damage to the mucous membrane.

Other long-term effects of cocaine use include long-lasting inability to sleep, heart disease (which could lead to heart attacks), and the increased risk of strokes.

Cocaine-withdrawal symptoms

When a cocaine user stops using the substance abruptly, he or she experiences what is termed a "crash" or withdrawal symptoms. This results in an extremely strong craving for more cocaine. It also results in fatigue (being tired), loss of pleasure in life, depression, anxiety, irritability, and sometimes paranoia. These withdrawal symptoms often prompt the user to seek more cocaine.

Chapter 11

ALCOHOL:
The socially accepted killer

A lcohol (ethanol) is represented by the chemical formula C_2H_5OH. A colourless, volatile and flammable liquid, it is synthesised or obtained by fermentation of sugars and starches.

Alcoholic drinks have been prepared and drunk for thousands of years. In fact, the use of alcohol is so widespread worldwide it is unimaginable to think that society can at any period in time completely rid itself of alcoholic drinks.

It is true that the great majority of alcohol drinkers can be described as responsible drinkers, who may on occasion take a sip of alcohol, then stay away from it for a while before returning to it on another occasion. The problem though is that what usually begins as moderate consumption can, in the case of some individuals, escalate in time to excesses and, yes, lead to addiction! Indeed, a glass of liquor drank by someone today may lead that person to drink two glasses tomorrow, then three, four, five, etc., on subsequent days... and before that person realises it, he/she is caught in the tentacles of alcohol addiction.

When consumed, about 20 per cent of the quantity is absorbed through the stomach; the remaining 80 per cent through the small intestine. Once in the bloodstream, alcohol is distributed to all parts of the body. It is eventually broken down in the liver into less harmful substances.

Initially, alcohol exercises a suppressing effect on the central nervous system, leading the consumer to feel more relaxed and cheerful. It also enables the consumer to shrug off their inhibitions.

WHY DO PEOPLE DRINK ALCOHOL?

In a previous chapter, I outlined some of the factors that could lead one to become addicted to some of the substances under consideration. Though what was said there is valid for substances of abuse in general, there are some additional factors unique to alcohol.

Socialisation: Studies have shown that the main reason why people consume alcohol is for socialisation. Many people drink as their way to fit in with others. It often boosts their confidence and helps reduce stresses they may usually have in a social setting.

Taste: The reason given by many to explain their drinking habit is because of their likeness for the taste of the alcoholic drink in question.

Relaxation: Some drink to relax, or feel at ease. One of the problems with this is that many people get used to feeling at ease and relaxed and start to rely on alcohol to make them feel that way on a daily basis. At this point, the reliance on alcohol can eventually turn into an addiction, which can lead to destructive behaviours and health problems.

Just to get drunk: Though they belong to a small proportion of drinkers, there are those who drink just for the sake of getting drunk.

Because everyone else is drinking: There are others who drink for the simple reason that everyone else is doing it.

Misconception about the effects of alcohol on the user: In certain societies, people drink alcohol out of misconception about its alleged benefits to the body. In my native Ghana, for example, many associate alcohol with the following:

- Medicinal benefits: helping for example in the cure of chicken pox.
- Male potency: it is believed to have a favourable influence on male potency.
- Sedative: it is thought to act as a sedative that can restore sleep to the person experiencing sleep disturbance.
- Appetiser: alcohol is regarded as an appetiser prior to a meal, or as a beverage that can help restore appetite.

HARMFUL EFFECTS OF ALCOHOL ON THE BODY

Mouth and oral cavity: Chronic alcohol consumption can lead to cancers of the mouth, the gullet and also the trachea (wind pipe).

Stomach: Alcohol can lead to chronic gastritis, which, if not treated, could in turn lead to the development of stomach cancer.

Pancreas: Alcohol may adversely affect the pancreas. The pancreas is an organ in the body responsible among other things for the production of digestive enzymes and also insulin. Insulin regulates the sugar levels in our body. Chronic alcohol intake can lead to damage to the pancreas, which could adversely affect the production of insulin, which in turn could lead to insulin deficiency and eventually diabetes.

Liver: Alcohol is broken down in the liver. Chronic alcohol use can adversely affect the liver leading to cirrhosis, fatty liver, hepatitis and liver cancer. By adversely affecting the liver, alcohol could impair the function of the liver in the production of digestive enzymes, clotting factors and cells needed in the defence of the body. These in turn could lead to impairment of the body's ability to absorb proteins, fats, and fat-soluble vitamins, as well as lower the defence capability of the body.

Damage to the liver can have a detrimental effect on blood circulation. In time, this could result in congestion in the flow of blood through the liver, leading to the development of varicose veins in the gullet or oesophagus. The varicose veins could rupture (burst), resulting in severe bleeding and, in some cases, the death of the affected person.

Heart: Long-term alcohol consumption can lead to a disorder known as alcoholic cardiomyopathy. In this situation, the heart muscles are weakened and as a result unable to pump blood efficiently.

Impotence or other sexual problems: Chronic alcoholism could also lead to impotency and other sexual problems, the details of which are beyond the realm of this book.

Central nervous system: Chronic alcoholism can adversely affect the brain in particular and the central nervous system in general. It can among other things impair memory, reasoning and judgement.

Effect of alcohol on pregnancy: Women who drink while pregnant could give birth to children suffering from a range of disorders known as foetal alcohol spectrum disorders (FASD). The most severe form of FASDs is foetal alcohol syndrome (FAS). A baby born with FAS can have serious handicaps and therefore could require a lifetime of special care.

SOCIAL, FINANCIAL AND OTHER CONSEQUENCES
Apart from the health problems outlined above, chronic alcohol consumption could have serious social and financial consequences on the individual involved. These include family breakdown, job loss, collapse of business, etc. Driving under the influence of alcohol could lead to accidents, in some cases severe road traffic accidents with resulting loss of life.

ALCOHOL-WITHDRAWAL SYMPTOMS
Alcohol-withdrawal symptoms usually set in within 5 to 10 hours after the last drink, but can occur days later. Symptoms get worse in 48 to 72 hours, and may persist for weeks.

The following are some of the symptoms of alcohol withdrawal:

- Headache—general, pulsating
- Sweating, especially the palms of the hands or the face
- Nausea and vomiting
- Loss of appetite
- Insomnia (inability to sleep)
- Rapid heartbeat
- Clammy (unpleasantly cold and sticky) skin
- Shakes (abnormal movements)

- Tremor, especially of the hands
- Involuntary, abnormal movements of the eyelids.

Delirium tremens: This is a severe form of alcohol withdrawal. Some of the symptoms associated with the condition are:
- Agitation
- Severe confusion
- Hallucination
- Fever
- Seizures, or epileptic fits.

Delirium tremens is a medical emergency that requires the admission of the patient to a hospital, not to a normal ward, but rather to the intensive care unit (ICU). The patient may need to be put into a sedated state (medically induced sleeping) for a week or more until withdrawal is complete.

Chapter 12

PRESCRIPTION DRUGS:
Meant for our good, but subject to abuse

I shall now turn my attention to the abuse of prescription drugs. These are substances that are prescribed by doctors to cure various conditions, but which unfortunately have the tendency of being abused. In the end they could lead to addiction and in case of abstinence cause the same withdrawal symptoms described for the substances touched on so far in this book.

The most commonly abused prescribed forms of medication are pain killers and tranquilisers. The pain killers commonly abused are those referred to as opiates such as codeine. They act on the body in a similar manner as heroin.

The next group of prescribed drugs that are widely abused are those referred to as tranquilisers. They are used to reduce anxiety, fear, tension, agitation, etc. There are two groups of tranquilisers, the major and minor. Examples of major tranquilisers are haloperidol and chlorpromazine. The minor tranquilisers are a group of medication known as benzodiazepines.

BENZODIAZEPINES

There are more than 15 different types of benzodiazepines. These include alprazolam, chlordiazepoxide, diazepam, and lorazepam.

They act to slow down the actions of the central nervous system. In appropriate dosage, they may help induce sleep, calm down, relieve anxiety and relax muscles. They can also be administered to a person experiencing an epileptic fit, to alleviate the situation.

This book will concentrate on diazepam. Also popularly known as valium, it is the most commonly abused substance in the group. A doctor may prescribe it to help with sleep, calm down the anxious, relieve muscle spasm, etc.

Its ability to help with sleep and relieve anxiety leads others to resort to it. In the end they may become addicted to it.

Those who abuse stimulant drugs such as cocaine and ecstasy may also use diazepam to help them 'come down'.

Diazepam-withdrawal symptoms

As in the case of other substances of abuse, long-term diazepam use generally leads to tolerance or dependence. An abrupt stoppage of its use could among other things lead to the following:

- Insomnia
- Anxiety
- Panic attacks
- Depression
- Tremors
- Agitation etc.

PART FOUR

TREATMENT OF ADDICTION

Chapter 13

GENERAL PRINCIPLES OF ADDICTION THERAPY

P revention is better than cure, so the old adage goes. When it comes to the issue of substances of abuse, the saying becomes even more relevant. As I have stressed on several occasions in this book, those who have not as yet got themselves involved in any of the substances dealt with in this book are best advised to keep their hands off them, for once one becomes addicted to them it is extremely difficult, if not impossible, to be cured of the addiction.

Since we live in an imperfect world, unfortunately there will be individuals who, despite all warnings, may become addicted to one or more of the substances under consideration.

There may also be someone reading this book who, though not directly affected, may have a relative, friend or close associate who is affected. Such an individual or individuals may want to know the treatment options available for people who have already fallen prey to one or more of the substances dealt with in this book.

As I said at the beginning, we can, with the use of medication, cure some of the common ailments afflicting us. The matter is not that clear-cut when it comes to the issue of substance abuse.

As we saw earlier, the substances concerned affect the mind—not only by impacting on the brain reward system but also in affecting the brain chemistry in various ways.

Indeed, cure for a person addicted to some of the substances of abuse treated in this book does not usually come easily, but is instead a gruelling, painstaking process, a situation that calls for patience, determination and perseverance not only from the directly affected individual but also from all involved—medical personnel, close family members, friends, etc.

Indeed, a typical addict usually requires long-term care, which will not be devoid of relapses, to achieve the end goal of a drug-free lifestyle, a situation that in turn could lead the affected person to become reintegrated into society, learn a trade, find work, build a family, etc.

There are two aspects of drug treatment: (1) use of medication; (2) behaviour therapy.

Medication: The first step in the therapy of drug addiction is detoxification. Depending on the substance in question, various forms of medication are employed. Currently, there are medications for the detoxification of heroin, nicotine and alcohol addicts. At the present time, however, there are no such medications for treating withdrawal symptoms arising from the other substances treated in this book.

Earlier on, I explained the term poly-drug abuse. Most people with severe addiction problems are poly-drug users. Such individuals usually need to take a different medication at the same time to prevent the onset of withdrawal symptoms typical for the different substance in question.

Behaviour therapy: As I mentioned earlier, drug addiction can also be described as a problem of the mind. The substitution tablets may prevent physical withdrawal symptoms. They cannot affect the psychological aspect, however. That is where behaviour therapy comes in.

Behaviour therapy has the goal of modifying or changing the attitudes and behaviour of the affected individual toward drug abuse and of encouraging him or her to live a healthy lifestyle away from drugs. Behaviour therapy can enhance the effectiveness of medications and help people stay in treatment longer.

Chapter 14

WEAPONS IN THE FIGHT AGAINST ALCOHOL, HEROIN AND NICOTINE ADDICTION

In this chapter, I will look briefly at the treatment options available for alcohol, heroin and nicotine addiction.

Alcohol: The first step in alcohol addiction therapy is detoxification.

The benzodiazepines diazepam (valium) and chlordiazepoxide (librium)—not given together—are employed. They are usually given over several days. The daily dosage is gradually reduced over several days and then stopped completely after a while.

As I stated earlier, alcohol withdrawal symptoms can be life-threatening. As a result alcohol detoxification is usually carried out under close medical supervision. Individuals with a history of heavy alcohol usage and also individuals with alcohol problems and underlying medical conditions are usually admitted into hospital and treated as in-patients.

On the other hand, individuals who are not heavily addicted to alcohol, who are only at risk of mild to moderate withdrawal symptoms, can be detoxified as outpatients.

Detoxification is followed by behaviour therapy. In the process the affected person is counselled on the necessary steps he or she could take to bring a change in his or her attitude towards alcohol. Behaviour therapy may be offered in groups or on an individual basis.

Heroin: Methadone, buprenorphine and naltrexone are examples of medication used in the treatment of heroin addiction. These medications act on the same targets in the brain as heroin and so help to suppress withdrawal symptoms and relieve cravings.

Nicotine: To help individuals addicted to cigarettes overcome their addiction, a variety of formulations containing nicotine in different concentrations are employed in what is known as nicotine replacement therapy (NRT). These include the nicotine patch (like a wound plaster, it is fixed to the skin for a period of time), nicotine spray, nicotine gum, and nicotine lozenges.

These contain nicotine in various dosages. The person wishing to overcome his/her addiction needs to take or apply them to the body as the case may be for a period of time. The aim of therapy is gradually to reduce the concentration of nicotine supplied to the brain over a period of time so as to prevent withdrawal symptoms and in so doing to help the addict quit his/her habit.

Apart from the above formulations, certain medications, for example bupropion and varenicline, are available in the treatment of nicotine addiction.

In addition to these measures, behaviour therapy including group and individual therapies are employed.

PART FIVE

REAL LIFE STORIES

I n this section, I will briefly describe a few of the several cases relating to people suffering from substance abuse I have come across as a medical doctor, particularly doing work as a prison doctor. I am not doing this to gain any advantage. Instead, I am narrating these life stories to serve as a warning to others.

A saying in *Twi* has it that "he or she who is behind needs to learn from those who have gone before them". It is indeed my hope that those who *are behind*, after reading about the experiences of some who have *gone before*, will learn from them, indeed, and allow their experiences to serve as a warning to them.

Chapter 15

THE NEAR-DEATH ENCOUNTER OF
A YOUNG ADDICT

During my time as a student at the Hanover Medical School in Germany, I used to work as a ward assistant on various wards of the teaching hospital during the weekends and holidays. The job offered me an opportunity not only to earn money but also to gain some experience in the field of nursing.

One could be asked to perform various duties as a ward assistant. These included dressing the beds of patients, washing patients not in the position to do so themselves, distributing meals, taking the temperature as well as the blood pressure of patients, etc.

The medical student employed to offer a helping hand to the nurses on the wards could also be asked to do what was known in German as *sitzwache*. Translated into English, the term means literally, "sitting awake" or "keeping watch".

The person employed to do a *sitzwache* was required to keep constant watch over patients whose condition, while not considered life-threatening enough to require admission on the intensive care unit, still required someone to watch over them around the clock.

The following are some of the conditions that could necessitate the engagement of a *sitzwache*: patients who were considered at risk of harming themselves; patients suffering from severe alcohol-withdrawal symptoms; patients who after undergoing anaesthesia were confused and were at risk of pulling out their IV lines or catheters etc.

One Saturday morning I had just got up from bed and was preparing to go shopping when my telephone began to ring. The voice at the other end of the line led me to guess what could be in store for me. It was the voice of Miss Franke. She manned a recruitment centre specially set up by the hospital to recruit at short notice medical students and other health professionals to fill unexpected shortfalls on the nursing staff rota resulting from sudden illness or other unforeseen circumstances.

"Good morning," she greeted in her usually friendly voice.

"Good morning," I replied.

"We need your help..."

"How can I help you at this early hour of the day?" I interrupted her.

"You certainly can guess why I am calling."

"You need me to work, eh?"

"Yes indeed!"

"Where are you sending me?"

"To Ward 25, one of the medical wards."

"One of the nurses has reported sick?"

"No, we just need extra staff."

"What is the matter?"

"It is the case of a young drug addict who has threatened suicide. She has been put under constant watch. Not long ago, a patient jumped to her death from an open window. We want to prevent a repetition. Please help us; I have spent the last half hour making several calls. No one seems to want to help me."

After considering the offer for a while, I decided to accept it. Though it would interrupt my plans for the day, the money to be earned was worth the sacrifice.

Although several years have since passed, my encounter with the patient, a young woman aged about 19 years, is still fresh in my memory. A few days prior to our meeting she had been found lying unconscious in the ladies' toilet at the central railway station of Hanover. The paraphernalia that were found beside her—a syringe to which a needle was attached, a small spoon, a tuft of cotton, a powdered substance and a lighter, led the alerted paramedics to suspect a possible overdose of heroin, a suspicion that was later confirmed.

Happily the immediate attempt at resuscitation produced favourable results as she began to show signs of revival. Next she was rushed to the main teaching hospital of the city and admitted to the intensive care unit. Thankfully she continued to make good progress after her admission.

After keeping her on the ICU over a few days, she was transferred to the normal ward. The decision to place her on constant watch was taken after she attempted to harm herself on the ICU.

To prevent her from going into heroin withdrawal, the doctors had prescribed her alternative medication that was dispensed to her at regular intervals. One would have expected that as a result of her near-death encounter a few days earlier, she would take her mind off heroin. Earlier I wrote about psychological dependence. Indeed, though she was receiving substitute medication to prevent her from undergoing physical withdrawal, that did not help keep her mind off the substance. Instead, she kept demanding from the nursing staff and myself that we supplied her with "stuff", as she termed it.

I was employed to keep watch over her a few more times. About a week after her transfer to the normal ward, she was discharged from the hospital. Even as I write, I ask myself what became of her. Was she able to overcome her addiction? Or has she, as in the case of several others addicted to heroin, in the meantime met her untimely death?

Chapter 16

THE ONE-LEGGED PRISONER

N ext I want to report on the case of a young man of about 20 years who I met in a prison in England. Because he had reoffended on so many occasions in the past he was regarded by many in the prison as a "regular visitor" rather than a usual prison inmate.

When I first met him, I felt so much sympathy for him. I really began to wonder whether indeed he was fit to be in prison in the first place. One may wonder what led me to that conclusion. Well, the young man in question boasted only one leg, the other one having been amputated a few years before. In several instances when doctors amputate a limb, the amputee is provided with a prosthetic limb to compensate for the loss. In the case of the young man in question, the amputation was carried out very high up the thigh, not far from the groin, a situation that made it impossible for him to wear a prosthetic limb. Thus the only way he could move around was by means of a pair of crutches.

When I first saw him, among the prison inmates, I wondered what on earth had brought him to the situation in which he found himself behind bars. In the course of time, the reason became clear to me—he had been caught shoplifting. I asked him why he had done that. He needed money for "stuff", he declared, somewhat unrepentant.

Later I had time to interview him, to get further details about him and also to find out what had led to the amputation of his limb. The following is the gist of what I learnt.

He became addicted to heroin when he was about 15 years old. Initially he had been injecting into the arm veins. As is usually the case with heroin addicts who introduce the substance into their bodies in that manner, a time came when the veins of the arms became damaged to the extent that he could no longer inject into them.

At that point, he began to look for alternatives. In the end he settled on the large veins of the groin. Unfortunately, in the process the great vessels of the thigh became damaged to the extent that the doctors saw no other alternative than to amputate the affected limb.

One would have thought that having gone through that harrowing experience he would put his addiction behind him. Well, deep in his heart, he might indeed have wished he could! Unfortunately, as I have stressed on several occasions in this book, once one has become hooked on a substance such as heroin, it becomes very difficult to free oneself from its influence.

Chapter 17

THE MIDDLE-AGED MAN FORCED
TO DRINK DISINFECTANTS

T he following conversation that I had with a prisoner aged
about 60 years occupied my mind for a long time.

"What brought you to prison?" I wanted to know.
"Theft, Doc, theft!" was the reply.
"What did you steal?"
"Alcohol!"
"Yes indeed?"
"Yes."
"Why did you do that?"
"You should know, Doc!"
"What should I know?"
"That as a person addicted to alcohol, I need alcohol on a
daily basis!"
"But that should not lead you to steal it!"
"Well, if I happen to have the means, I purchase it from
the next available shop. If on the other hand I do not have the
means to do so on a certain day, I roam the shops until I find a
favourable opportunity to steal."

"But there are CCTV (closed circuit television) cameras all over the place."

"Never mind the cameras! In several instances, I am able not only to outwit the cameras but also the security at the exit. Well, that is not always the case, otherwise you wouldn't be interviewing me in prison today."

"What happens on the days that you are neither able to buy nor steal alcohol?"

"In that case, I head for the local hospital!"

"For the hospital? What has the hospital got to do with your search for alcohol"

"There are disinfectants hanging about in the corridors of the hospitals!"

"What are you driving at?"

"Well, as you know, hospital disinfectants contain alcohol! I just look for a favourable moment when no one is watching, remove them and hide them in my coat. Back home I dilute it in water and use it as a substitute for alcohol."

"That can't be true! Disinfectants are not meant for human consumption!"

"Alcohol is alcohol, Doc!" he concluded.

Chapter 18

THE DOCTOR WHO WENT ON A RAMPAGE

One day as I worked as a prison doctor in the UK, a highly respected medical doctor came to prison on remand. His offence? Here we go:

1. Under the influence of alcohol he threatened to kill his wife and their two daughters with a kitchen knife.
2. Scared to death, the threatened wife called the police. Moments later the sirens of the approaching police vehicles filled the air. Before their arrival, the drunken man ran into the street, armed with the kitchen knife.
3. Soon he came across a young woman about to get into her vehicle. With his knife pointing at the frightened lady, he demanded she hand him the car keys. Soon he was fleeing from the police in the "stolen" vehicle. The police gave chase.
4. As he fled he rammed the vehicle into several other parked cars on the street. In the end he was arrested.
5. At the time I met him, he was on a 24-hour watch due to the threat of suicide.

The solicitors and other legal experts among us may want to sit down to list the number of possible offences committed by this learned and noble fellow. Indeed, when I met him, I just could not imagine that the decent looking individual sitting before me could commit the offences he was charged with. He himself, now freed from the influence of alcohol, could also not fathom what he had done.

Chapter 19

THE SUCCESS STORY THAT ENDED
WITH A PRISON SENTENCE

A well-established native of Ghana resident in the UK also had his story to tell when I met him in prison. On account of previous driving offences relating to alcohol, he had been banned from driving. A few days prior to our meeting, he had attended a party that his company had thrown to celebrate a lucrative contract they had won. He could, in his own words, not resist the urge to drink.

He should have taken a taxi home instead of choosing to drive his own vehicle. As he drove home, probably as a result of his erratic driving style, he was stopped by the police. Soon the officers discovered he was not only driving in a drunken state but that he was not permitted to drive in the first place. He was arrested on the spot and eventually arraigned before a judge. His lawyers pleaded with the judge for clemency and offered to pay a substantial fine in return for a suspended sentence.

The court refused to accept the deal and sent him to prison instead. Although it involved a short sentence, the fact that he had been sent to prison at all was devastating for him. His prison sentence would forever serve as a dent on his reputation; henceforth, he would be burdened with a criminal record.

I can go on narrating personal tragedies involving victims of various substances of abuse until the cows come home. The reader may have their own accounts to add to the unending lists of the harm, embarrassment, trouble, disgrace, etc., that the use of some of the substances listed in this book can bring to those who are addicted to them—yes, those who, unfortunately, have become enslaved to substances that, at the end of the day, are ordinary, innate matter that human beings are expected to have dominion over in the first place.

www.ingramcontent.com/pod-product-compliance
Lightning Source LLC
Chambersburg PA
CBHW030109070426
42448CB00036B/591